# Indiana
# Hill Country
# Poems

## NORBERT KRAPF

DOS MADRES
2019

# DOS MADRES PRESS INC.

P.O.Box 294, Loveland, Ohio 45140

www.dosmadres.com    editor@dosmadres.com

Dos Madres is dedicated to the belief that the small press is essential to the vitality of contemporary literature as a carrier of the new voice, as well as the older, sometimes forgotten voices of the past. And in an ever more virtual world, to the creation of fine books pleasing to the eye and hand.

Dos Madres is named in honor of Vera Murphy and Libbie Hughes, the "Dos Madres" whose contributions have made this press possible.

Dos Madres Press, Inc. is an Ohio Not For Profit Corporation and a 501 (c) (3) qualified public charity. Contributions are tax deductible.

Executive Editor: Robert J. Murphy

Illustration & Book Design: Elizabeth H. Murphy
www.illusionstudios.net

Author Photo © Richard Fields

Images in this book are adapted from paintings by Emmanuel Zairis and Alfred Sisley which are all in the public domain.

Typeset in Adobe Iowan Old Style

ISBN 978-1-948017-50-3

Library of Congress Control Number: 2019944626

*First Edition*

# ACKNOWLEDGEMENTS

The following poems, sometimes with different titles and often revised, originally appeared in:

*Connotation Press: An Online Artifact:* "Garip and the Clouds," "In the Spirit House";

*Flying Island:* "Ash Wednesday and Valentine's Day," "Big Soul Sister," "No Knockin' at Heaven's Door," "Queen Anne Reflections," "Radio Song of the Bees," "Scorpio Wrecking Ball," "Stillborn Lovesong," "The Altar in the Kitchen," "To Come Knockin' at Your Door";

*From the Edge of the Prairie:* "Across the Ohio," "Down the Alley," "Flow, River, Flow," "Five and Dime," "Ohio River Panorama," "Sunday at the Lake";

*So It Goes:* "All Soul's Blessing," "Redneck Love Song," "The Lost Art of Listen";

*Ramshackle Review:* "The Catfish and the Poem";

*The Seventh Quarry* (Wales): "Franconian Fields";

*Tipton Poetry Journal:* "Abe's World," "Hometown Solo Walk," "Indiana Shadows and Light";

*Valparaiso Poetry Review:* "Hearing Poems Read in Franconian Dialect."


Thanks to the editors of the following anthologies in which these poems appeared:

*Airmail from the Airpoets* (San Francisco Bay Press, 2011): "All Soul's Day, Erlangen," "Moon Lover," "Southern Indiana Nocturnal";

*Cowboys & Cocktails: Poetry from the True Grit Saloon* (Brick Street Poetry Inc., 2019): "Grandpa Benno on the Karl May Express";

*Indiana at 200: A Celebration of the Hoosier State* (Indiana Bicentennial Committee, 2016): "A Prost to Our Roots";

*Naturally Yours: Poems and Short Stories About Indiana State Parks and Reservoir, 2013:* "Spirit of Hills and Woods";

*The Best of Flying Island* (Indiana Writers Center, 2015):
"Scorpio Wrecking Ball."

Former Louisiana Poet Laureate Darrell Bourque read, on his
radio poetry program at The University of Louisiana Lafayette,
KRV, Radio Acadie, from "Prophetic Ancestors."

Thanks to the editors of all these magazines, anthologies,
Indiana Bicentennial publications, and the radio program for
giving these poems a place to breathe in a previous life. Thanks
also to John Matthias for sharing with me the beauty of Dos
Madres Press publications.

And thanks to Richard Fields, my collaborator on *Songs in
Sepia and Black and White* (Indiana University Press, 2012),
who holds the copyright on the author photo used on the
About the Author page.

*for Elfrieda and Leon Fleck,*
*Jasper cousins and friends,*

*and in memory of*
*Mary Lou, my sister*

# TABLE OF CONTENTS

## I. Hill Country Poetics

## II.  A Prost to Our Roots

## III.  Entering Lampert's Woods

Loyalty to place arises from sources deeper than narcissism. It arises from our need to be at home on the earth. We marry ourselves to the creation by knowing and cherishing a particular place.

—Scott Russel Sanders,
*Staying Put*

I simply want to make the claim that the mind is formed by the shape of the land, by the sheer geography of the mind's physical location. And the shape of the mind, under the influence of the land, will yield a particular kind of poem with a particular kind of expression.

—Maurice Manning,
interview in *Matchbox*

# I.

## Hill Country Poetics

## Patoka River Invocation

Muddy water, muddy water,
flow with your brown silt,
at the bottom of which
dark carp glide and suck.

Patoka, Patoka, river
of my youth, on the banks
of which still stand silver
maple, cottonwood, sycamore,

you rose and raged in the spring,
swelled onto the low streets
in Frog Town and lapped at
the bottoms of crawling cars,

put us back in our place,
then shriveled to a puddle
and a trickle in the dog days
of August and came to a stop.

Stand still, stand still, Patoka,
spirit of all that once was here,
stream of all I came to be,
but flow, flow on after I go.

# The Catfish and the Poem

Like a catfish, I love bottom,
need both earth and water, feel
around with my whiskers. I do rise
toward the surface but always turn
back down. When I am hooked
and pulled up out of my element,
I heave and gasp in air where water
should be, like a heart pumping
but cut off from arteries, a poem
with no reader to channel blood into,
a denizen of the depths turned ugly
and lame in a shock of sunlight.

# A Dream of Parents

Such a simple dream it was,
of a mother who grew up
on a farm she brought

with her to the small town
and kept the garden growing
behind the house at the edge

of the woods being logged
as the house was being built
with her flowers blossoming

red, pink, white, iris blue
all around it; and the father
born in a village where all

the folks farmed and his father
ran the steam engine sawmill
and threshing machine

and always stories of that life
came with them and blue grapes
growing around two sides

of the vegetable garden
for the wine that fermented
in the cellar in the basement.

This was the dream I inherited
from them of life in the country,
of having vegetables and flowers

and fruit trees always growing
around you and following
the turn of the seasons

harvesting hickory nuts and walnuts
in the forest in the fall to crack
and pick and eat in the winter

and hunting and fishing
in ponds and the river
and trapping in fields

and canebrakes and listening
to the songs of the birds
that came to eat our berries

and seeds and sang us into
the next good day breaking
with the light that fell on us.

# They Twine in Green

I see them in their garden
where they dance their wordless
waltz with ease and green grace.

He sharpens the hoe
and loosens soil around shoots.
She pulls weeds loose.

He pushes the hand plow
down long mounds of dark
loam to open the trench

into which he places white
spuds. She feels the peas
swelling in their pods.

He ties tomatoes to stakes.
She digs up shallots she
inherited from her grandparents.

Sweet potatoes are his specialty.
Rhubarb around the borders
of the garden is hers. They

meet somewhere in the middle.
Everything they touch grows.
Their spirits twine in green.

# The Altar in the Kitchen

The pink carcasses of rabbits
and fox squirrels shriveled in pans
of salted water in the sink.

Sometimes cleaned bluegill,
sunfish, or catfish settled
in round bowls of water.

Baking pans of rhubarb,
blackberry and apple cobbler
cooled on the north window sill.

Ball jars of peaches jiggled
in boiling water on the stove
to winter in the cellar.

The kitchen was our Grand Central,
the table our stark altar,
and the priest, the farm girl

who gave birth to us, fed us,
nursed us back to health,
prayed over us in storms.

## Particles of Life

There were shelf mushrooms
growing on the bark of trees
and the sounds of cicadas,

bits of hickory shells free-
falling through layers of leaves
illuminated by sunlight,

the cawing of a crow
farther back in the woods
that kept opening into depths

of valleys and ridges
and streams slowly sliding
across flat-rock beds

as I took my silent steps
as a boy alive with sight,
sound and a sacred sense

of might be, should happen,
and could come true, and ever
growing possibilities that

did not end with just me
but pulsated and vibrated
with particles of life beyond.

## Our Lady of the Peace

When my father returned from
Our Lady of the Peace Hospital
in Louisville after they shot

electricity through him
to calm his nerves, he sat
in the white oak rocker

they told me his father
sat in holding and rocking me
before he died when I was

still a toddler. I sat
a few feet away
from him on the couch.

I was maybe sixteen.
My father's pastor, his
spiritual advisor, had

sexually abused me
and probably at least
fifty other very sad boys.

I looked over at Dad
as tears slowly leaked
out of his eyes and slid

down his cheeks.
No sound in the room
except for the rocking

of those white oak runners
across the rug. I wanted
to cry but no tears came.

I wanted to say something,
like, "You'll be all right,"
but no words came.

For all eternity, I will be
sitting there with my father
watching those tears leak

out of his soft blue eyes.
There is a letter from him
to Mom I found in a drawer

after she died, eighteen years
after he did, in which he told
her from Our Lady of the Peace

that he was all right but his
gums were very sore from
all that electricity he felt.

My eyes are dry now
and my gums are shrunken
as the tissue pulls away

from the teeth, which
I take care of as best
I can in my mid-seventies,

and that white oak rocker
is always never far away
from where I write.

# Down the Alley

When I was a child I loved to walk
in our working-class neighborhood.
Our fathers worked in wood factories
and made chairs, desks, cabinets.

My favorite was to walk down
the alley that sloped from our house
to Great Aunt Mayme's. I would
pick out the vegetables in gardens

and name tomatoes, peas, beans
squash, beets, and rows of white
potato blossoms. When I reached
the back yard of Aunt Mayme's house,

it was always as if she had been
waiting for me to arrive. She said
my name, made me feel welcome,
and gave me a glass of sweet tea.

I almost never saw anything but
a smile on her face. Uncle Joe,
whose words came slowly, also
smiled, but in a different way.

I could tell his attention came
from some other place, put light
on my focused face, and left
me at the center of his gaze.

Now, most of a lifetime later,
I try to be like them, giving
rapt attention to green plants
growing and people who are

in their small ways trying to find
whatever makes life interesting
and beautiful and blesses their
being in this world with us.

# Five and Dime

Way back then I used to wander
into the Five and Dime on the Square
right across from the Court House

all by myself. It didn't take much
moolah to buy what I wanted,
a little bag of warm cashews with just

the right amount of oil and salt. I would
start chewing and savoring those warm
morsels before I was out the door without

a thought of sharing one single nut.
I didn't own very much but right then
I had all that I needed and knew what

it meant to be content. I was beholden
to nobody but grateful to the woman
who served me with such a sweet

and understanding smile because
she knew what she was giving me,
how much I would enjoy it, and also

how innocent I was. Probably she
was a mama herself and maybe she
had a daughter she wished I would

one day meet. That Five and Dime
has been gone for a long time
and no doubt that smiling woman

is nowhere to be found except when
at a party I pick out just the right
cashews from the dish and I'm back

there looking up with small coins
in my hand to give in exchange for
my salty bag of delights and a smile.

# Grandpa Benno on the Karl May Express

One winter in southern Indiana, my Grandpa Benno
shut down his steam-engine sawmill and threshing
machine and this time headed out from St. Henry

for the Wild West and time on Easy Street, Texas,
where large saloons were always open and Cowboy
Cocktails were ready to be imbibed. How did he get

there from southern Indiana? My father, born above
a saloon across the street from the village church,
said his father headed down the road to the nearby

Johnsville Station, caught the Karl May Express,
and rocked the rails West down to Texas all by his
lonesome. Dad said he sent postcards back home

telling folks he loved their winter weather and those
lip-smackin' good Cowboy Cocktails he sipped
instead of the beer he quaffed in that saloon run

by his father-in-law, August Luebbehusen. Let's say
those cocktails were a winter treat for Grandpa Benno.
He claimed in a postcard one, not a Manhattan, made

his mustache tingle! He gave its name as a Maiden's
Kiss. How could it not tingle if you see the recipe
he wrote down in a handwriting suspiciously like

old German script: first a Maraschino, then Crème
de Roses, White Curacao, Yellow Chartreuse,
and some Benedictine the monks served

at St. Meinrad Archabbey just down the road
from St. Henry. You go try a Maiden's Kiss
and tell me it won't make your white 'stache

turn black again! Try and tell me such a cocktail
won't make you rock down the rails on the Karl
May Express sitting in the white-oak rocking chair

you made by yourself and relax, to devour the fiction
of Karl May in German and tales about the friendship
between white cowboy Old Surehand and Winnetou,

Chief of the Apaches. Don't complain that young
Karl May, of poor weavers, went to prison for stealing
six candles and stole a watch and lost his teaching license,

then started to write well-researched best-selling novels
depicting brotherhood between races and championed
world peace. Though he never made it to the Wild West,

he reached Buffalo, New York. Look, I believe in
the imagination and the pen as power tools for
brotherhood and harmony. Just a minute, dear reader,

here comes that A Maiden's Kiss I ordered. My gray
mustache has started to tingle. Sit yourself down! I
ordered it for you. *Ja!* Here's the Karl May Express!

# The Dark Red Heart

Mine is the voice
that arises in the middle
of the dark night
to speak in your ear.

What I say comes
to me from a source
I do not see
but beats like
a heart that is as
dark red as the stone
I hold in my hand.

Jasper, it is called,
also the name
of the town
in the hills in which
I was born at night,
in the dark.

My fingertips touch
the smooth surface
of the heart I hold
and rejoice when they
come to the rough
indentations near the top.

I would touch and hold
and sing my song of
all that is smooth
as well as rough
and let the beat
of my red heart

pulse in the poems
that come in the night
and beat toward
the coming light

with the love
of place and people
and the blood
of the land.

# Spirit of Hills and Woods

(Brown County State Park)

I am the voice
of hills and woods.

In me you hear
the cry of the red-tail hawk
riding a thermal

and the gray squirrel
barking in the branches
of the shagbark hickory.

I am the deer
bounding over the hill
and the rabbit
crouching in briars.

I drift like the crimson leaves
of the sugar maple
and float on the waters
of creeks and ponds.

I bubble up out of rich
humus deep in the woods
from an eternal spring.

## Hill Country Poetics

So it's true then
all the way back when

I shelled peas from the pod
into a pan beneath the sugar maple

I was thumb-flicking out
the essence of an experience

into a shape that would
hold and contain it

and saving the nourishment
to savor and digest another day

and if that ain't the same
my friend as making a poem

and somebody ingesting its
essence I don't know what is.

# Dialect Poetics

When you say something in a different way
in a different kind of speech or tongue

you do not say the same thing you said before.
Walt Whitman did not find a new kind

of spoken American English to say what
other poets already said. He took us into new

territory by finding a new kind of language.
James Whitcomb Riley did not make up

farm boy dialect to express the reality of urban life.
He didn't speak like a backroads hick because he

didn't know the language that poets spoke in
to one another and put into books because

books were for the learned. He knew the people
and the life of the people who came from the farm

and wanted to go back there for one reason or another
and he knew the life they had left behind but also

brought with them. Grammarians do not make
the best readers of poetry and if you smell shit

and call it feces you might please some folk
by not making them smell it but by God

you'll lose others because they'll wonder where
you came from and why you're so afraid of what

stinks but which all animals including humans drop
down into one kind or another of hole most days

and must admit came from her or his self
but it goes way beyond that and comes to a way

of thinking and feeling and laughing and crying
that needs the right language to make you feel the same

and keep or rediscover how the people you know
and love talk to one another when they're alone and need

to say something they all understand and must share
to be on common ground and speak from the same heart.

# When Abe's Mama Took Sick

What you think it was like
when his mama took sick?

You believe the boy didn't know?
That little big boy who was nine?

He didn't remember how
they crossed over the big

river from Kentucky on a ferry?
Left the old place behind?

Didn't remember his
mama's voice reading him

and his sister stories from
the Good Book on Sundays?

When she had to lie down
and couldn't get up no more,

how did it feel to look
at her and wonder how long?

How could he not cry even
if his tears found no voice?

How could his mind not go
there when he sat worrying

in the White House as all those
soldiers lay dying in the fields?

When he wrote those words
saying the dead consecrate

the land by giving their lives
so that the union might endure,

did he not flash back to his
mama who taught him in a cabin

how to read and write
and make him see

how holy a word can be?
Did he not wonder if the mama

who cooked him and his sister
food in the cabin looked down

on him and his family as they
lived in a house so big filled

with the spirits of the men
and women who first made

the country what it is?
Did the tall man who kept

so much hidden beneath
his big top hat not go back

often in his thoughts to
the time when his mama

who gave him the gift
of learning to read and write

had to lay herself down
for the last time and no

words that came together
in a prayer no matter how

sacred could ever help her
get back up and walk again?

## Stillborn Love Song

I love you when
the dusk thickens,
evening falls in every
direction, and the dove
coos ever more forlorn.

I love you when
October air turns crisp
and smoke rises like
the breath of angels
from the chimneys.

I love you, stillborn sister,
when everything turns so quiet
the only sound I can almost hear
is the settling of snowflakes
on branches above my head.

I love you most when
All Souls Day returns
and the veil between
your world and mine lifts

and your spirit breath
drifts back down to earth
and touches these lips
waiting for your kiss.

# Redneck Love Song

1.
Mama's back home
hangin' out the wash
while daddy's in the woods
takin' a break from
workin' in the fields.
That shotgun you hear
blastin' at squirrels
fits his right shoulder.

2.
My brother's overseas
fightin' in jungles for
what I can no longer tell
and mama can't hardly
listen to the news
for fear of what she
might learn about
what's happened to him.

3.
When you love a place
you can't leave it
just because of a war
no matter what folks say.
Sooner leave behind the girl
you fell for the first time
you saw her stroll down
the road in pink short shorts.

# Moon Lover

Sometimes I lie communing
with the moon whose full
light keeps me awake,
but when she rides up
and moves above me,
I feel her mystical weight
settle down and our rhythms
become one. That faint
smile you sometimes see
catching the corners of these
lips is a rune written
in marks she left on me
when she went away just as
daylight followed her spin
and brightened her to invisible,
leaving me with a vision
of beauty and a tongue
that only hints of the love
we made and left behind
for you to decipher.

# Scorpio Wrecking Ball

I'm your Scorpio wrecking ball,
the red pepper in your soup,
the flash of pain in your belly.

Oh I can sing it intense,
I got the gut-bucket blues
deep down in my psyche

but I can see the stars
when they flash and sometimes
I climb the ladder higher and higher.

If you're the one listens well
I'll sneak into your office and let
my roiling guts spill in your truth chair.

I bet you'll even smile ever so slow
and sweet and offer me herbal tea.
That's when I go ballistic, baby,

quoting the prophets and visionaries
before you put a hand on my shoulder
and tap me into good-boy submission.

Come on outside and we'll howl together
in harmony at the full moon over our heads
before it's time to head back to the cabin.

You wouldn't believe how calm
I can become when the time is right.
Sit with me, stare into my animal eyes.

# Queen Anne Reflections

*for Sarah*

We were gathered in a Queen Anne house
moved along roads that wound through woods
to a site on an open hill surrounded by trees.

No walls on the main floor. Just exposed
two-by-fours with art hanging from studs.
Tables with covers and fresh flowers set up

in café style. Pitch-in food in the basement.
Beer and wine brought along to share.
A pianist and I brought jazz and poetry

with a soft southern Indiana accent.
We all floated together free of gravity.
As I half sang, half-chanted, and recited

my poems, a young woman with long
curly hair seated almost within reach
looked and listened with the quiet

intensity of a plant sending out tendrils.
A white light radiated from within her.
She looked familiar and of the place,

but shone like a local mystery.
You could tell by the look in her eye
that she had something to give, but

not a gift that calls attention to itself.
She knew how to look and listen,
to absorb what she saw and heard.

It was clear that she was growing
into whatever powers would be hers.
Vision and voice were coming near.

# Southern Indiana Nocturnal

In the woods an owl screeches.
Racoon eyes glow in moonlight.
The lights extinguish in the farmhouse.
The rock road tucks around the barn
and snakes into the lower forty.
The winding lanes of crushed white
rock give off ghostly demarcations.
Under a cluster of trees, deep
in the woods, the plumbing
of a still has separated and rusts.

# Over the Hill

It was the hour
not long after dawn
when light pulled away

from the dark
and my mother
was still sucking

in breath with pain
as I was walking
up a hill

near the woods
where I hunted
squirrels as a boy

and I looked up
and saw one
small hill away

three young deer
bounding like spirits
toward the crest

and it was as though
they were leaping
into the pale moon

and then they
were gone leaving
not a trace

except in memory
where so many live
and I knew

the time had come
for me to let go
and let her live

in that world
beneath my eyelids
where spirit

is present crossing
back and forth
over the hill.

# In the Spirit House

Even when I was young I did
not think of cemeteries as sad.
To me they were quiet and peaceful
and housed spirits of those I loved.

When I became a father I often
brought my children to a cemetery
landscaped like a rural park.
We brought along a picnic lunch

and ate it and drank juice on a stone bench.
Sometimes we saw a rabbit or a pheasant
between tombstones. Periodically a diesel
commuter train ran along the back of the plot.

We played games and read books and I
pronounced the names carved in stone.
That world was populated with spirits
who became our friends, not enemies.

We did not walk in fear or dread.
We enjoyed the privacy of our park.
Nobody told us to go away.
Nobody told us to be quiet.

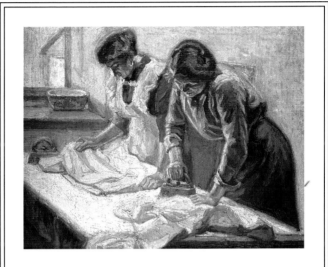

# II.

## A Prost to Our Roots

# A Prost to Our Roots

When we came here, we were full of dreams
and did not let reality kill them. We buried too
soon too many of our young and elders but kept
working, clearing, planting, praying in German.
If our prayers were in German, our ambition was
American: good land, a house we built with our
hands of timber we cut down with an axe, crops
in fields we cleared and plowed, cattle in barns.
A church we built of Indiana sandstone pulled on
sleds by oxen from a farm beside the Patoka River,
near the bridge and the mill we took over built by
Scots-Irish Presbyterian. Some of them moved on
when we came in. The Croatian missionary Rev.
Kundek, who spoke our native language, but not
so well as us, sold us government land, looked
after our needs, marched like a general at the head
of our parades, built our court house, advised us
how to vote and do business to stay together as a
small German Catholic colony. The Benedictines
from Einsiedeln, Switzerland took over for the
Little General when he died. We built factories
in which we made chairs, desks, fine cabinets,
organs and pianos. The love of music has always
been with us, even when shade from the forest
still flooded in through our windows and open
cabin doors.

Now we have brick houses, straight streets,
vegetables growing in gardens, flowers bloom-
ing in beds surrounding our houses and in boxes

hanging on the railings of the concrete bridge over the Patoka. Our Strassenfest celebrates our heritage in red, gold, and black and polkas in the summer. The church bells in our landmark Romanesque church with the Tower of London still peal and toll in the center of town. Basketball hoops hang from every garage. We keep our cemeteries well cut and trimmed and care for our ancestors' tombstones carved in German script with the names of the Bavarian and Baden towns they came from and wanted us to remember. We know where we came from but love it here where we stayed. Some of our young have learned how to speak the old tongue that was verboten during two world wars, and we have a sister city in southern Germany, a little town from which some of our ancestors came. We go there, they come here. Our taverns serve frosted schooners of beer that go down easy in the summer and we like our schnapps in the winter. A Prost to our roots all these years later!

# Prophetic Ancestors

*for Darrell Bourque, former*
*Louisiana Poet Laureate*

## 1. Prophetic Ancestors

Even when we break through
into an area we find new
we are tied at the center
to what we left behind.

In our speech breathe
words and rhythms
that cling as relics
of past rite and ritual.

The features of our faces
are embedded in the lines
of old tintypes and photos
of forebears long departed.

We are the ghosts
of who we used to be
and the prophetic ancestors
of what we shall become.

## 2. Always a Place

Always a place to have to leave
and another to find and come to.
So many leavings and left behinds.
So many yearnings, so many regrets

and griefs, such a deep need to
put down roots and stay put.


## 3. The Right Place

When the right place comes
to us we open to it.

Everything that grows and bends
in the breezes and moves and
speaks in its own language,
its silent medium of expression,

says this is it, the place
where you were meant to come
and be and stay and love
and give all of yourself to a future
you make and build for all

you hope will remember not just you
but all who came in spirit with you.


## 4. What a Place Says

The right place speaks to us
in a language we've never spoken
but remember hearing from
some other life elsewhere.

Stay here, is what it says,
in different words,
over and over, in variations
that deepen the message
we were waiting to hear.

My earth, my plants, my
animals, my sun, soil, air.

From here I move no more.
Here I will sing my last hymn.
Here I will leave my mortal remains.

# Franconian Fields

Where the rich soil
lies turned to the sun
by the point of the plow
I once walked in the fields.

Where the leaves
turn yellow and red
I once walked in woods.

Where the church steeple
in the next village
points into the sky
I once prayed.

When I walk
these fields and woods
every step springs
a thousand affections

and a worn lane
leads to a house
where I once lived.

## Franconian Cemetery Scene

From the edge
of the woods
I watch a man
kneel before a new
tomb and carve
with a battery-
driven tool.

I guide his hand
to write my name
clearly and simply
on the top of the marble
page and on the bottom
help him conclude:
*Read my poems!*

# All Saints' Day, Erlangen

Whorls of gentian blue
beam bright between green

spikes and dark brown
linden leaves in the botanical

garden as the veil between
us and spirits stretches thin,

weather turns gray and raw,
and moisture assumes the shape

of snowflakes to descend
and ride on our shoulders.

# Garip and the Clouds

*for Helmut and Garip*

In the back of his Erlangen grocery store behind
a screen at a table with a miniature Turkish
carpet and a dish of figs, dates, apricots and grapes
Garip reads, at our request, a poem. He tells how

he came into the world buck naked and so
he would not freeze, his mother reached
for a tattered blanket, found none, and wrapped
him in clouds. Ever since then, the clouds

have pulled him along and he is somewhere
between clouds and deep blue seas, between
Asia and Europe. "Don't ask me about home.
Do the clouds or the deep blue sea claim me?

Do I belong here or there?" He brings us a bottle
of Turkish wine called Villa Doloca made of a grape
named The Eye of the Ox, and we drink until we float
between continents like clouds drifting in the wind.

Together we toast a life lived between continents
and countries where wine and poetry and music
and food bring people together and make time
stop at the intersections where human life begins.

# Kristina and the Scarves on the Bridge

Kristina comes to the bridge in Nuremberg
and sets up her scarves of many hues and textures
that call out to people passing by and draws them
over to stand and look and talk and feel

the right color and she knows but doesn't
say it aloud just quietly suggests this one
wants to wrap around the tender skin
of your neck and speak to the shades of colors

in yes your eyes but you should look around
there are scarves of many colors will speak to you.
*Ja Ja!* I can make change oh this one looks good
on you goes with that but you must decide you

are the one must know what is good for you.
I remember you the last time you came from
so far away yes I remember your daughter
with the dark eyes who is so friendly she

lives here now oh yes I remember when you
came before and found that dark navy blue one
with the almost closed white circles that looked
like Pictish stone carvings oh so sorry you lost it!

That was the only one of its kind somebody
must be happy wearing it now and you will find
another one to suit you. Well I don't usually let
people take my picture, I always look so stupid,

but okay, yes, you can take one of me with your wife.
I remember you and your wife and daughter
and now the dark eyes of the baby grandson
you showed me so pretty yes until the next time.

# Grandson in the German Woods at Four

In the woods my grandson puts
his tummy on the forest floor

and looks around. He sees
the curving shapes of leaves

and sunlight splashing
onto and between them

dripping onto the earth
and himself. He rests

his hands on his round
Franconian cheeks, looks

out and around with dark
Colombian moon eyes

as his free American spirit
soars upward and out toward

all creatures and shapes
he senses himself a part of

and knows like a little Buddha
how rich is the life he feels.

# You Stand There Ironing

*after Tillie Olsen*

You stand there in the den ironing
elegant onesies you bought cheap
at the retail outlets on New Year's Day
for our grandson Peyton to mail to him in a red,

white and blue Priority Mail box to Germany
where he is discovering the powers of observing
the world from the watch tower of his high chair.
You smile as if caught in your own pleasure dome

in front of the gas fireplace in our downtown
townhouse in this Midwestern city.
Behind you in a large framed photo stands
a Franconian farmer, Hans Engel, an angel

of the fields where my day-laborer ancestors
worked before emigrating to America.
Above him on a shelf stands another
framed photo of three farm women sweeping

the streets of their village clean for the weekend.
I smell the steamy heat of my mother's iron
and hear her hum as she finds new places
to put a crease in our clothes and see your mother

stir smothered eggplant in a big iron pot
on the stove above a blue gas flame
in her Louisiana kitchen. Into these several
houses walks Tillie Olsen holding a pen to stand

with all our mothers as you stand with all our
grandchildren who will step into their freshly
pressed clothes and walk into the world just as we
fade away into the memories that live for them.

# Indiana Shadows and Light

## 1. Southern Indiana

Into the woods I came to listen
so I could see. My father
heard but I saw better.
Droppings of hickory shells

said squirrels before a tail appeared.
Came to know names of shagbark hickory,
white oak, walnut, beech, pig hickory
as food trees. Stepped lightly toe first

so no dry leaf or branch said a thing.
Always looked up, ears wide open.
From him I learned beauty, shapes
of trunks and branches, configurations

of leaf clusters and flash of red tail
that said fox squirrel. Some trees
and woods older than others,
immersed in ancient shadow.

Entering time outside of time.
Feeling connected with oldest of ways.
Shade deepening into darkening dusk.
Bird tweet and whisper as late prayers

remaining from a time before I came
to be born. Before I could hear
and see. Before words came into
my mouth for tongue to taste.

## 2. On the Edge of the Prairie

Four hours by car to the north
on the edge of the prairie
I came into the life of books.
Sometimes rode the Monon

from the hills of the south
into land that looked and felt flat
though it did begin to undulate
and wind could howl and whip

like I had never heard or felt.
Heard the blab of wheels
on pavement and felt the splendid
silent sun on my slender shoulders

in the pages of Walt Whitman's
Leaves of Grass. Saw corn grow
in every direction. Baptized in green.
Consecrated and confirmed in the lines

of poems. Walked away with a piece
of paper said I was educated. Felt good
but I knew better. Knew a beginning
was far from an end, no way a conclusion.

## 3. South Bend, Golden Dome

Came upon a Golden Dome
and a Touchdown Jesus
in mosaics on the outside wall
of a library that became my home.

Met and lost one young woman
and found another in the basement
beneath the stacks where grad students
stood and scarfed hot or cold lunch

bought from vending machines
that dropped packaged food
that tasted stale and inert.
Talked books, lit crit, more books

and listened to young Dylan
and the old Delta blues, the blues
that came up to Chicago. Reborn
in the blues. Poetry in song.

Song in Beethoven, too,
in the choral movement of the Ninth.
But the poems would not begin
until the last degree was finished.

Blues came East with me,
along with a Cajun bride.
On the North Shore of an Island
off the East Coast poems came

to sing of southern Indiana woods
and hills, of hickory and walnut
and white oak and fox squirrels
and elders who spoke in German.

# Song of the Radio Bees

Back then when Indy was a world away to the north
I was a teenager in Kentuckiana washing and waxing

cars and drinking beer with chums when the engines
sounded on the radio like wild bees in the woods

swarming nearer and nearer as a loud hum
turned deafening and they roared closer.

When I first sat in the grandstand decades
later as a man circling into his seventies

I heard a female voice say, "Ladies and gentlemen
start your engines" and those bees roared again,

louder than ever before. The low-slung cars
roared off, big bumps raised on my arms

and legs, and my lips smacked with the taste
of honey and malt as this late song brewed.

# The Canal to Evansville

after a letter of 1838 in the
Indiana History Center Archives

## 1.

We got to get this done, he said.
Get that canal from Terre Haute
all the way down to Evansville.
This is our highway, you know.
Let's take it over to Worthington
along the White River to Evansville.

The Irish are good, but if
time becomes our enemy,
lets hire some Germans.
That will surely push
the good old competition.
*Arbeit, Arbeit, das macht
man frei, ja?* Get it done!

The canal in Evansville
is already constructed.
We only have to join to it
out in the Wesselman Woods.

## 2.

How in Hell were we to know
the railroad would come in
so damned soon? We did our
very best. Maybe one day
a boy from Jasper will ride
over a little bridge above what

was once a canal and wonder
who built it, what it was like
to work on it, and dream of
riding on a canal boat.

Maybe the water level will
be low and the weeds high.
Maybe this boy won't know we were
blind to what was coming our way.

# Spinning Cincinnati, Ferdinand, St. Henry, and Jasper Baseball

after an 1839 letter of Charles Mayer
sent from Indianapolis to Stuttgart


In Cincinnati in Over-the-Rhine
you could get almost everything:
brown sugar, brandy, tea
in big bags and barrels.

Like many others, we came there
from what's now Germany and then
left for parts more unknown...

Went down the Ohio
by flatboat to Troy hauling
along packed in old trunks
heirloom bibles and dishes
and glasses from the Old World
and up a corduroy road to
Dubois County, where land
was being sold and cleared.

Bought land to farm not far from
the new town of Ferdinand, founded
by the Archduke of nearby Jasper,
Rev. Joseph Kundek of Croatia,
colonizer of German Catholics
in the hilly, shadowy wilderness.

Yes, we built a brick
farmhouse on a hill just over
the line in Spencer County.

After the Civil War when
the nearby village of St. Henry
came into existence, we moved there
and August Luebbehusen built
a tavern with living quarters above
where my father was born and learned
how to sip beer sitting on the lap
of his grandpa. Saw teamsters
from the nearby St. John Station
with their wagons full of goods
pull in and order Brats and Bier.

Lots of folks in St. Henry had once
lived in Cincinnati, in Over-the-Rhine.
Lots of Jasper folks too. By the landmark
Romanesque St. Joseph Church built
by German pioneers in the center of Jasper,
the neighborhood was once upon a time
called "Little Cincinnati" where Bier,
Brats, and baseball were popular.

That boy who learned to sip beer
on his grandpa's knee in the tavern
in St. Henry played baseball for
the St. Henry Indians and Sundays
pitched for them in the pasture.

Later he taught his first son,
the one who became a poet,
how to throw a mean curveball
in the alley behind the garden
in Sunset Terrace, Little Kentucky,
on the outskirts of Jasper.

For every time the boy threw
one that curved sharply after
he put the right spin on the ball
his daddy gave him a sip of beer
and taught him also how to
put a spin on any story he told.

# Where I Come From

From deep in the hills in a holler
where the screech owl screams
in the darkest hour of the night.

Everywhere in the woods where
so many pairs of eyes burn bright
until the dawn creeps in to settle.

From back in the corner of the woods
where a still once cooked the white juice
that goes down hard and bitter clean.

Where thunder claps and lightning flashes.
Where hard rain hits the earth and runs
in channels choked with leaves and debris.

Somewhere in the far field where
an old tractor rattles up and down
the rises pulling an ancient plow.

Inside the barn in which a work horse
stomps and whinnies raring for light
of day to break and oats to chomp.

In kitchens and cellars where women
cook and can and clean and sweat
to prepare food and guffaw from the gut.

Everywhere old men gather to spit
tobacco into a bucket and tell tales
of what they've seen in their days.

That barnyard over there where a rooster
crows as if to curse the forces and defy
all obstacles daring to block his will.

Where the coonhound at night barks his
heavy canine blues as he aches to roam
unchained in the wild woods of his dreams.

# Abe's Worlds

Backwoods but brilliant,
he traipsed the trails from
Kentucky to Indiana to Illinois,

and then on to Washington.
He knew equally well
the Shakespeare soliloquy

and the crude backwoods joke.
The difference between the pig sty
and the federal government

was disappointingly small.
Both were swamps but one
was infested with men.

## What's Deepest

What's deepest in us speaks
through us when the time
is right: the memory

of a turtle dove cooing
from an evergreen branch
at the back of the garden,

the falling of the star-shaped
leaf turned red that lands
on the wooden picnic table,

the black stain of the walnut
husk that colored our fingertips
black to remind us of where

we came from and what we valued
most when we were young, the way
that morning sunshine found

our face and called us to the promise
of a new day that might bring us
to the life we dreamed about

but were not sure we could ever
find no matter how hard we tried
to make it all our very own.

# The Dead Come Knocking

I have heard the dead come knocking
in the middle of the night, softly.

You have to be listening alertly
to hear the sound in the silence.

They knock only when they know
someone is listening and interested

in seeing them up close. Once I let
them in and they entered like cats

happy to find a friend and rubbed
up against my leg, purring. I will

not divulge their names but will admit
two of them acted strikingly like

my mother and father. They sat together
like individuals who love one another

and were happy to be near me again.
Their eyes were brighter than those

of the others and I thought I could see
glimmers of a smile behind their whiskers.

Yes, I reached down to touch them
and whispered, "So good to see you

again! You are always welcome here.
My door is always open for the two

of you. You know I sleep very lightly,
sometimes hardly at all. Just purr

and I will welcome you in again!
I see you often in my dreams."

# All Soul's Day Blessing

Bless the baseball cards I thought I saved,
rubber bands holding them in a box,
hunched in the attic, with batting averages

of my favorite players stored in the attic
of my memory. Bless the red leather cap
with lined ear flaps I wore all day Saturdays

in November and December, even in January,
hunting rabbits and quail with the bird dogs
Queenie and Ike. Bless the .22 rifle and .410

and .16 gauge shotguns I balanced on my shoulder
walking into woods and staring up at branches
of tall and shaggy hickory trees on which I could

have lived the rest of my life. Bless the baby sister
Marilyn who was born dead just a month or so after
I turned six but who seems more alive than many

people I know. Bless the brother who moved away
fourteen years ago without saying a word and refuses
to answer any mail we keep sending him though I

told him his beloved sister has leukemia. How can
I beg him better to be in touch with her? Can't he
see what a lift one word from him would give her?

Bless my mother and father living in us who love
them and carry them in our hearts and souls as we
step more gingerly every day. Bless our poor son

who has an illness of the mind that can't take away
the beautiful heart that keeps beating in his chest.
Bless our daughter and her husband for giving us

the little grandson who smiles, talks, laughs
and snickers in German and English and calls me
Opa and his grandmother Oka for Katherine/Oma.

Bless the light but ever-present spirits and souls
whom we lost but still have with us on this day
when the veil between worlds is so thin and sheer.

# The Lost Ritual of Listen

Sometimes I am thirsty
for silence and need
to drink deeply of it.

Everywhere we turn
TV, radio, barber shop,
comes static, angry noise.

What happened to listen?
When did it go extinct?
Where did the voice

of silence go when we
lost it? Is it still there?
Have we lost all ability

and desire to hear what
it has to tell us about
who and what we are?

Come stand with me
when the earth opens
each year and green

tips push out into the air.
Let us open both ears
and listen gently to

what this birth says
to us. Let us remember
to bring our children along

so they may inherit
the lost ritual of listen.
For millennia our predecessors

understood and spoke
this language of silence
and passed it along to

their youth. Why not us?
Why not listen as much
as we talk? Why not receive

and give this green tongue
of the earth to our young to
savor, hum, sing, and revere?

# In the Garden of Stories

When we return to our home place
a part of us sits in the room that was
once upon a time our upstairs bedroom
and looks out the window at the garden

in which vegetables like beans, peas,
potatoes, corn, squash and tomatoes grew.
We see rhubarb still growing around two
sides of the space that was humus rich

and peonies open their blossoms
after old tree trunks burned smoking
and depositing ash behind. At night
a part of us sleeps in the bed in which

we read Poe's The Tell Tale Heart
and the Cask of Amontillado that
kept our eyes open as we put a pillow
over our head to keep out evil spirits.

Mornings arrived with a new sky and a sun
hanging above bringing bright possibilities
that help us throw off our blankets and walk
down the stairs into the kitchen where the rest

of our life begins to open allowing us
to read and share books full of stories
and memories and pick up a pen and push it
across paper to recreate our relived stories

for others to read leading them back
to their houses set back into other woods
and gardens with vegetables and flowers
growing out of earth blossoming into story.

## Sometimes a Song

Sometimes a song comes back
from somewhere in your soul
and your mouth shapes the lyrics

once again and it's as if you
wrote it and sang it and pulled it
out of the depths of your psyche

about someone who may be gone
but comes back again and you see
that smile you remember and hear

the soft voice saying your name
in a way that makes you quiver
and a light that had gone dim

glows now and begins to burn
and you are somewhere else
with a sense of belonging

that gives you a voice to sing
and celebrate what you regretted
you had lost but recover and reclaim

giving you a sense of wholeness
you did not know you could reach
and share with others who return.

# III.

## Entering Lampert's Woods

# Heading South

Today I am heading south
into the hills I love
with my friend Helmut

who sees how much
the landscape is like
his native and my ancestral

Franconia. Tomorrow we
read our poems in his
language and also mine,

back and forth in turn.
Leaves fall and bare
the ribs of trees

standing like sentinels
as we pass by listening
to the music of the seasons

and give ourselves
to the dance of time
and the coming

celebrations of our
births in my November
and his December.

# Hometown Solo Walk

I like to walk the streets
before dawn opens an eye
on the day. Even when damp

licks at the street
I love to put my feet
where none have gone

before me on the new day.
There is something that pulls
me in the dark all the way

to the landmark Romanesque
church and behind it
into the cemetery where

the ancestors who came over
and my stillborn sister lie
looking up at whatever stars

burn well above the clouds.
There is something about seeing
in any degree of darkness

that brings one more deeply
into the center of things
and what spins within.

# Hearing Poems Read
## in My Ancestral Dialect

Hearing poems read in Franconian dialect
brings back memories of the past
in a language old but not suspect,
in words that deep down do last.

I still hear our mother and father
talking at table when we were young
in a language that did not falter
but in which we could not have sung.

Now when a friend from my ancestral region
reads earthy poems in words half familiar
it brings me back to that earlier season
when life was basic and rules were regular.

The human center of our life does not change
even if the words we speak evolve and range.

# Entering Lampert's Woods

I was nine when I followed
my father into the sweeping hills
and valleys of Lampert's Woods
with a .22 bolt action rifle

held in my hands as if it were
a baby with a mighty power
I had to cradle lest it go off
wrong and wreak havoc.

We first wound and careened high
up a dirt road that was crushed
red sandstone and parked
in a barnyard, put on our vests,

and started walking. Into what?
Majestic trees, shadows, shade.
Sounds of barnyard life receding
behind us. Language of insects,

trills of songbirds, raucous honk
of crows, barking of squirrels.
Mystery behind my eyelids. Sun-
light coming to shine and filter

sometimes, momentarily, on us
a little boy and his father let loose
in a world that was gloriously theirs
without any sense of ownership

because it was so deep and wide
and expansive, a secret sea within
that belonged to all but to no one
in particular, so huge, vast, endless.

To stand there, feeling so small,
so blessed to stand in the silence
but also enlarged, taken somewhere
beyond anything I had witnessed,

unaccountably rich and stepping
gently on the sacred loam rife with
the layers of years of decomposed
leaves, to feel that beneath the soles

of borrowed hunting shoes, to look up
and see and feel light from beyond, was
to be alive in a new way with eyes still
opening wide, given entry into the holy.

## Sunday at the Lake

It's Sunday at the lake
and everyone is in orbit
or frozen at the long table.

What and how much
to pile on your plate?
Where to sit and with

whom? How many relatives
can come together, eat,
nod off, go swimming,

shout, murmur, go silent,
walk around in twos
and threes, drift off

on pine boughs in shade,
hear mosquitos hum
and whine? From what

distant radio does Elvis
hound dog, shake us up,
and heartbreak our hotel?

Who fired the sun so hot?
How many snakes slumber
beneath the overturned

row boat to slither away
when we turn it upright
and hurl curses after them

before diving deep down
into the cool and murky
waters of Sunday infinity?

# The Tolling of the Bells

In the town where I was born
stands a big stone church
with a tall tower and the face

of a white clock with black numbers
and when someone died you could hear,
anywhere in the small Catholic town,

the tolling of those deep bells.
People came out of their houses
to look churchward and ask,

Who died, wonder who died?
In that church some priest
once upon a time poured water

on my head, another laid a wafer
on my tongue, and a bishop rubbed
oil on my forehead to confirm

I had become a full member
of the church making me part
of something larger than myself

for which I am still searching.
Now I wonder if those strong bells
or the bells of another church

will toll after my last breath and if
anyone will come out of a house
and ask who died, and I also wonder

if anyone will read the poems I wrote set
in that town and accept the truths I told
no matter how dark and deep they toll.

# Earth Song for Marilyn

Little sister
so quiet and
eternally patient

you are always
here when I
come back

to say hello,
still GONE TO
BE AN ANGEL

as your tiny
tombstone says.
This time I

bring a friend
from our
ancestral Franconia

who writes poems
and plays in our
ancestral dialect.

Helmut and I
walk from the
weathered stone

of our Schmitt
ancestor to yours
not far away

and across the street
and up the hill
over the crest

to where my
parents lie
and we know

the right
language to
say hello

beneath clouds
in the sky
through which

the sun shines
onto the grass
still green

though fall is
a comin' in
and winter

lies not so
far behind
in the earth.

# Ash Wednesday and Valentine's Day

Not long after we received ashes
on our foreheads, I learned from
my brother that our sister Mary

passed into spirit in her sleep last night.
No more sister suffering, no more
blood sister left in this world of flesh,

but a beautiful spirit remains always
a spirit beautiful in any and every world.
I was to see you in less than a week,

but now Mary I will see you always
alive, giving others hope and courage,
wanting always to lift others toward

the best they can become, believing
in what they would give to us. You gave
us eyes to see gifts hiding in ourselves.

# Mary in a White Lace Dress

You are there, a beautiful almost twenty-five.
It is your wedding day and you hold a bouquet
of white and gold flowers that match your
white-haired mother's dress on your left.

Your white-haired father, who died later
in November, stands on your left. Behind
and between you and your father stands
your oldest brother, with thick black hair

and beard. On your far left stand your
other two brothers, with hair and mustaches
that echo your reddish brown hair
that holds a tucked-in golden flower.

Your sister-in-law from Louisiana
remembers buying your white lacy dress
from Jeannie's Found Money thrift shop
in Roslyn, on the North Shore of Long Island,

and giving it to you, because you loved it
and her. And so you made it your wedding dress.
Somewhere nearby stands your Massachusetts
groom with a mustache. This is a day of suits,

vests, and ties for the men and your lacy white
dress, Mary. This is the only picture I remember
with all five members of our family standing
together. When your sister-in-law reminded me

of this dress, where it came from, how much
you loved it, and your decision to make it
your wedding dress, I saw you again
in the bloom of your beautiful youth as we

sat eating dinner in a restaurant on the evening
of the day you were transformed into pure spirit,
covered my face with a dark blue cloth napkin,
and wept tears of loss for the smile on your face.

## Sister Love

Mary, we are standing close together
in the Florida sunlight a few years ago.

There is light in and on your face.
I wear a borrowed blue baseball hat

and transitional progressive glasses
tinted a bit dark. Your strawberry blonde

hair is from our father's side of the family.
My hand rests happily on your shoulder.

Neither of us has to speak to say
what we feel about each other. Light

always knows where and when to shine
just as love knows where to find a home.

# No Knockin' on Heaven's Door

You didn't have to knock
on heaven's door, Mary.
You didn't have to knock.

Old Peter knew you were comin',
Mary. He knew you were comin'
and that door swung open wide.

When I told your nephew Daniel
you had passed into spirit,
he said to me on the phone:

I think Aunt Mary's in heaven,
don't you, Dad? I said to him:
I'm sure she is, son, oh yeah.

Aunt Mary didn't have to knock
on heaven's door because it
was already open wide for her.

Behind Peter stood Grandma Dots
and Grandpa Clarence and Mary's sister
Marilyn who never drew a single breath.

Aunt Mary never had to knock
on heaven's door cause it was
already swung wide, wide open

and she had more than paid
any dues she ever owed anybody
and she must have smiled when

she heard that heavenly choir
sing as she stepped out of that
high-flyin sweet old chariot.

# To Come Knockin' at Your Door?

Sister, every year you wrote to your
brother who cut off from all of us
and our children fourteen years ago

without telling us where he went
or why. You wanted to stay in touch.
Your husband dug up his address.

Sister, somebody hurt brother bad.
I know it was a priest about whom
a cousin sent me word that late in his

life he insisted he wasn't likely to go
to heaven because he had done "terrible
things." I know well what they were.

He did them to brother and he did them
to me. It's nothing you ever did to your
brother that kept him away so silent.

He never answered your letters or mine.
You told me late in your too short life
that you kept hoping he would one day

come knock on your door. I almost begged
him to knock knock on your door. As far as
I know, he did not, even though he was

fond of you. Sister, any brother who
cannot come knocking on your door
is hurt worse than we can ever know.

Some doors remain always open.
Like yours. He didn't even have to
knock. Your heart was always open.

# Sister Breath

Sister, sometimes I awake and see
your face smiling at me. It's hard
to believe you're gone from this

world in which I remain, while drawing
nearer to the one in which you live.
But I also see and feel you alive in me.

You have become not one smidgeon
less real to me. It may be you are
more real since I learned from a text

that you "passed." Oh sister Mary,
are we not all passing from one
state into another from the very

moment we are born until we
exhale our last breath? I still
hear your breath as clearly

as I hear my own. I see you present
with the diaphanous sister whose
breath stopped before it ever began,

stillborn Marilyn. I feel both of you
breathing within me, the only two
sisters I know inside our family,

though we all know there are many
more sisters who are part of us all.
So many breaths to listen to at night.

# Big Soul Sister

When I told a woman writer friend
about your rheumatoid arthritis
leading to a related type of leukemia,

Mary, but pointed out that your spirit
remained positive and you retained
an eye for the good in others,

she replied: "Sounds like your sister
had a body difficult to live in
but a big soul full of light."

## Outside of Time

Come back for a few minutes, Mary.
Come back for a few minutes, sister.
There are a few things I'd love to say.

One you've heard me say before.
I've also heard you say it to me.
One more time, Mary: I love you.

I still hear myself say it on the phone.
I still hear you say it back to me.
One more time, Mary, I say it to you.

I wish we could have been together
just one time in the last two years,
sister. I wish it could have happened.

Your poor body was breaking down
and our son was having his problems
but I never stopped thinking about you.

In four more days I would have seen you
but maybe I see you better now, Mary.
I still see your beautiful smile shine.

I still hear your sweet voice full of love.
I remember holding you in my arms
when it was time to fly back to Indiana.

I remember you waiting for us as we
landed in Florida during the Indiana winter
and seeing you stand there with a smile.

## Ohio River Panorama

They entered by flatboat
into this S-curve
I gaze down upon.

Trees and shade
and the unknown,
but also promise,

on every side.
What could they see
of what lay beyond?

Could the family
know they will
bury their father

in just three years
in my hometown?
Let's allow the wife

and six children
the faith and hope
that brought them

into this water curve
from so far away.
Let's allow them

to rejoice that they
have made it so far
and give thanks that

what they began
we pass on to
flow into others.

# They Are Here with Us

They are here in the sandwiches and chips we share
and the beer we sip after arriving from the cemetery.

They are alive in the memories we recount
to one another the first time we are together

after decades of being apart. They smile
as we tell stories about the time when

we didn't know who we were or what we
might become. Now we see how much

confidence they had in our future while
we yearned to escape their world into ours

whatever it might become. Oh how small we
were and how small they would grow when

they turned old. How young we felt but now
how old we know we too have suddenly grown.

And our young, how beautiful they are to us who
live for what they do and want for them what we

felt eluding us but realize they will give to us
as they see in our eyes how we love them.

How warm is the hug the young give us
as we say goodbye and thank them

for coming and how we all see ourselves
in one another and the common blood we feel.

# Across the Ohio

Squirrels, he wasn't sure
if fox or grays, or maybe
separate groups of both,

were coming across
from the ridges of Kentucky
into the hills of southern Indiana.

They were swimming across the water,
he told me. He knew an old farmer
who saw them coming in bunches.

Moving into the woods and bending
the branches of the tall trees.
You could see them coming

from far away, if you looked up
hard enough.  They would start
cutting on ripe hickory nuts

and strip a tree, leaving fresh
cuttings in a sacred circle
as if around an ancient altar.

I always accepted then what
my father said about the coming
of these creatures we revered,

because he passed on his faith.
He always believed it would happen,
was ready to receive this blessing.

This was our way of praying.
We talked about woods
that had squirrels in them,

or if they didn't right now,
soon would, after they passed
over on the waters of the Ohio.

We shared this watery epiphany,
this cornucopia of splashing
furry tails and chattering teeth.

All we had to do to see them
crossing on the river was close
our eyes and breathe deep.

Light descended on the waters,
treetops sagged, and hickory
cuttings drizzled from above.

# Rose Petals in New Harmony
*—for Karen & Jim*

1.
Rappites came here to clear
wilderness and build community.
Germans, lovers of things
well made and enduring.

Made gardens, grew flowers,
herbs. Lovers of roses, eternal
flames of red. Visions of harmony,
freedom, readers of the Bible.

Knew how to make solid buildings.
How to craft strong beer. How to
grow sturdy roses. Did not stay.
Went back to Pennsylvania.

2.
Karen and Jim came here
to commit to one another,
to join their love. Came with
family and friends and flowers.

Came with girls strewing
mystical red rose petals, left
and right, on concrete walkways
in Jane Owen's Roofless Church

in God's green out of doors.
Open to August sky. "Man
and nature belong together
in their created glory."

Light and rose petals everywhere.
We walked and we sang and we
listened to poems and gave praise
for summer sun and love. We looked

and saw an inverted rose built to give shelter
to a Jacque Lipchitz "Our Lady of Joy" sculpture.
Karen proceeded in a red dress carrying
red roses interspersed with a few whites.

Jim came and was waiting in a white
suit with red tie and boutonniere.
Kathleen of Texas and Eduardo
of Peru blended voices in song:

"My Way, My Truth, My Life,"
a hymn by George Herbert,
music by Ralph Vaughan Williams.
Tongues of angels, women, and men.

Ray, Onondaga, read an Iroquois
Thanksgiving Address; Joanna,
Polish Matron of Honor, wore sleeves
she crocheted and added for the wedding.

3.
Mrs. Red and Mr. White kissed
inside the inverted rose shelter.
Now they wore round rings.
Now we applauded and cheered.

Some took pictures. Some blew
bubbles. Everyone smiled.
Trumpets blew. Voices rose.
We all saw rose red and sang.

4.
Red canoes floating on the Wabash.
Red and pink surprise lilies blooming.
Champagne bubbling in our flutes
in the Red Geranium Restaurant.

Trees casting shade and surprise lilies
bow toward us from outside the windows.
We gaze into flame on every candle,
listen to toasts blossom on tongues.

We carry away with us everywhere
roses growing in Rappite gardens,
red lipstick on many smiling lips,
girls strewing red petal blessings.

# Morning Sylvan Symphony

One day I will come into a place
where trees live with their branches
stretching out over me. My morning

prayers will consist of looking up
into the early light sifting through
between leaves and listening to

the way they breathe and flutter
like semaphores of sacred meaning.
To stand there looking and listening

will be my liturgy of love. I want you,
dear reader, to join me there so we
can pray together. Too few understand

that how we pray is looking and listening
to what the trees say to one another.
This is the divine symphony that sounds

to any ears tuned to the scales and runs
of the forest. Let go of the clutter of busy
days and you will feel the music of gods

and goddesses speaking ever so softly
and then building to a stirring finale.
This is the religion of leaf, branch and bole.

Ignore it at your own peril, the poverty
of your soul, the shrinking of your spirit,
the shriveling of any love in your heart.

Open yourself and all your senses and feel
yourself grow immeasurably as all of your
single self joins with the surrounding swell

of a beauty that lifts you beyond yourself
to climb to the top where the breezes
help you sway to the rhythms you had

never felt until you let yourself wander
into this grove where all is aglow with
pure light and breath that transforms

you into sound and vision becoming
a hymn of praise that sounds from
within all the leaves surrounding you.

# Flow, River, Flow

River of my youth
winding through valleys,
wooded hills beyond
rolling on and on,
live in my song.

Flow, Patoka, flow.
Roll, hills, roll.
Stretch, valleys, stretch.
Sing, words, sing
so song may live.

Those who spoke
in the old tongue
left us their story
so we may know
the song of our origins.

Language of river,
language of valley,
language of hills,
language of ancestors,
sing in my song.

Song of my heart,
song of my people,
song of my place,
celebrate my love.
Love song, live on.

# ABOUT THE AUTHOR

 Former Indiana Poet Laureate NORBERT KRAPF was born in Jasper, Indiana in 1943 and has lived in Indianapolis since 2004. For 34 years he taught at Long Island University, where he directed the C.W. Post Poetry Center for 18 years. He has published twelve poetry collections, including *The Return of Sunshine*, about his Colombian-German American grandson, *Somewhere in Southern Indiana*, *Blue-Eyed Grass: Poems of Germany*, *Bittersweet Along the Expressway: Poems of Long Island*, *Bloodroot: Indiana Poems*, *The Country I Come From*, *Looking for God's Country*, and *Catholic Boy Blues*, which he adapted into a play of the same title performed at the Indy Eleven Theatre of IndyFringe.

Krapf has won the Lucille Medwick Memorial Award from the Poetry Society of America, a Glick Indiana Author Award for the body of his work, a Creative Renewal Fellowship from the Arts Council of Indianapolis to combine poetry and the blues, has had his poems included on IndyGo buses and a poem in stained glass at the Indianapolis International Airport and his poems read on The Writer's Almanac. He has released a poetry and jazz cd, *Imagine*, with pianist-composer Monika Herzig and collaborates with Indiana bluesman Gordon Bonham.

For the full Dos Madres Press catalog:
www.dosmadres.com